Faithful
Children's Leader Guide

Faithful:
Christmas Through the Eyes of Joseph

Faithful
978-1-5018-1408-2 *Hardcover with jacket*
978-1-5018-1409-9 *e-Book*
978-1-5018-1410-5 *Large Print*

Faithful: DVD
978-1-5018-1402-0

Faithful: Leader Guide
978-1-5018-1411-2
978-1-5018-1412-9 *e-Book*

Faithful: Youth Study Book
978-1-5018-1413-6
978-1-5018-1414-3 *e-Book*

Faithful: Children's Leader Guide
978-1-5018-1415-0

Also from Adam Hamilton

24 Hours That Changed the World	*Moses*
Christianity and World Religions	*Not a Silent Night*
Christianity's Family Tree	*Revival*
Confronting the Controversies	*Seeing Gray in a World of Black and White*
Creed	*Selling Swimsuits in the Arctic*
Enough	*Speaking Well*
Final Words from the Cross	*The Call*
Forgiveness	*The Journey*
Half Truths	*The Way*
John	*Unafraid*
Leading Beyond the Walls	*Unleashing the Word*
Love to Stay	*When Christians Get It Wrong*
Making Sense of the Bible	*Why?*

For more information, visit www.AdamHamilton.org

ADAM HAMILTON

FAITHFUL

CHRISTMAS THROUGH THE EYES OF
JOSEPH

Children's Leader Guide
By Nick Ransom

Abingdon Press / Nashville

Faithful
Christmas Through the Eyes of Joseph
Children's Leader Guide

This book is printed on elemental chlorine-free paper.
978-1-5018-1415-0

17 18 19 20 21 22 23 24 25 26—10 9 8 7 6 5 4 3 2 1
MANUFACTURED IN THE UNITED STATES OF AMERICA

Contents

To the Leader

This children's leader guide is designed for use with Adam Hamilton's book *Faithful: Christmas Through the Eyes of Joseph*. This guide includes four lessons that teach children about Joseph's life, Joseph's role in Jesus' life, and what Joseph means for all of us. The four lessons tell Joseph's story through the birth of Jesus, and a fifth lesson is included for groups that want to know what happened after Jesus was born.

The subjects for the lessons parallel the subjects in the program's adult and youth studies. Because of this feature, families will be able to discuss, across grade levels, what they have learned in each session.

The lessons in this guide, designed for children in kindergarten through sixth grade, are presented in a large group/small group format. Children begin with time spent at activity centers, followed by time together as a large group. Children end the lesson in small groups determined by grade level. Each lesson plan contains the following sections:

Focus for the Teacher

The information in this section will provide you with background information about the week's lesson. Use this section for your own study as you prepare.

Explore Interest Groups

In this section you'll find ideas for a variety of activity centers. The activities will prepare the children to hear the Bible story. Allow the children to choose one or more of the activities that interest them. Each activity requires an adult leader, so you'll need to limit the number of activity centers to the number of leaders you have. If you have one leader, select one activity for the entire group.

Large Group

The children will come together as one large group to hear the Scripture and story for the week. This section begins with a transition activity, followed by another activity that relates to the story or Bible verse.

Small Groups

Children are divided into grade-level groups for small group time. Depending on the size of your class, you may need to have more than one group for each grade level. It is recommended that each small group contain no more than twelve children.

Younger Children
The activities in this section are designed for children in grades K-2.

Older Children
The activities in this section are designed for children in grades 3-6.

Reproducible Pages

At the end of each lesson are reproducible pages, to be photocopied and handed out for all the children to use during that lesson's activities.

Schedule

Many churches have weeknight programs that include intergenerational gathering time and age-level classes. Here is one way to organize a weeknight program.

5:30	Meal
6:00	Intergenerational gathering introducing weekly themes and places for the lesson. This time may include presentations, skits, music, and opening or closing prayers.
6:15–7:30	Classes for children, youth, and adults.

Churches may want to do this study as a Sunday school program. The following schedule takes into account a shorter class time, which is the norm for Sunday-morning programs.

10 minutes	Intergenerational gathering
45 minutes	Classes for children, youth, and adults

Choose a schedule that works best for your congregation and its Christian-education programs. Blessings to you and the children as you explore the life of Joseph!

1 Meet Joseph the Carpenter

Objectives	Bible Story
The children will:	Jesus Returns Home
• Meet Joseph, the earthly father of Jesus	Matthew 13:54-56
• Learn what *humility* means	**Bible Verse**
• See the humility of Joseph and Jesus and try to practice humility in their lives	Don't do anything for selfish purposes, but with humility think of others as better than yourselves. (Philippians 2:3)

Focus for the Teacher

Happy Advent! Christmas is almost here! Are you ready? If you are like most people, you are probably saying, "No, I'm not ready! How can it almost be Christmas?" Well, don't freak out! Advent is here to help you get ready. In this series, we will look at the life of Joseph, Jesus' earthly father, and see what we can learn about Christmas through him. You'll notice that not much is mentioned about Joseph in the Bible, so we'll do a little reading between the lines. It is my prayer that this different look at Christmas will bless you and the children you'll be leading during the four weeks of Advent.

Let's get started with Joseph. Joseph, we know for sure, was a carpenter. He probably worked with wood and created items such as tool handles or other pieces of furniture. He probably was very skilled and worked hard. I'm guessing his business did not bring him many accolades, but it did provide

> Practice humility this week.

for his family. We'll see early in the Christmas story that Joseph's life was turned upside down when he learned from his fiancée, Mary, that she was pregnant with the Messiah. After the initial shock, Joseph was willing to set aside his own plans so God's plans could be fulfilled. I'm struck by the humility of Joseph, a hard-working carpenter who allowed the wishes of God, Mary, and Jesus to take precedence in his life while he took a back seat. Fast forward thirty years to Jesus' ministry, when he showed great humility. Part of me wonders if Jesus saw humility modeled by his dad, Joseph.

In this lesson, we'll begin the Christmas story and focus on Joseph's humility. We'll ask the children to put others first this Advent season, following the example of the humble carpenter, Joseph.

Explore Interest Groups

Be sure that adult leaders are waiting when the first child arrives. Greet and welcome each child. Get the children involved in an activity that interests them and introduces the theme for the day's activities.

Build It!

- As the children arrive, divide them into groups of two or three and give each group five minutes or so to create something out of popsicle sticks, toothpicks, and a few pieces of tape. (You can leave this experience wide open and allow them to be creative, or you can guide the children by asking them to construct a symbol of Christmas, build the highest tower, or something else you come up with.)

- *Note*: Creations don't necessarily have to be built up vertically; they can be horizontal on the ground or a table if you have enough space.

- Give children a two-minute and then a one-minute warning and then call time when they need to be finished. This helps everyone be finished at the same time, keeps children focused, and keeps the activity from dragging on too long.

- Walk about the room and take time to check out and comment on each group's creation. Then ask these questions:

    o   What name do we give people who build things with wood? *(carpenter)*

    o   Does anyone know any carpenters? *(Allow responses.)*

    o   Can anyone name a famous carpenter from the Bible? *(Joseph, the father of Jesus)*

- **Say:** Joseph, the earthly father of Jesus, was a carpenter. He built things out of wood—probably tool handles, furniture, and the like. Most people think Joseph taught Jesus how to be a carpenter when Jesus was growing up. As we begin getting ready for Christmas, we are going to look at the Christmas story through the eyes of Joseph to see what we can learn about God through Joseph.

- **Say:** Today begins the season of Advent. *(Write the word* Advent *on the board.)* Advent is a time we get ready for Christmas by thinking again about the Christmas story!

Prepare

✓ Supplies needed: popsicle sticks, toothpicks, tape, whiteboard or large sheet of paper, something to write with

Prepare

✓ Supplies needed: crayons, markers, whiteboard or large sheet of paper, something to write with

✓ Go to **Reproducible 1a: When I Grow Up!** at the end of this session and make enough copies for everyone in the group to have one.

When I Grow Up!

- As children arrive, hand them a copy of **Reproducible 1a: When I Grow Up!** and some crayons or markers to draw with. Give them five minutes to write and draw an idea of what they want to be when they grow up.

- If they have more than one idea, it's fine for them to draw all of them.

- Give the group two-minute and one-minute warnings. Call time and bring the children back together.

- Allow children to share their worksheets as time allows.

- **Ask:**
  o How would you feel if these plans you just created got changed?
  o How would you feel if God was the one who changed the plans?
  o Do you think God's plans for your life are the same as your plans for your life?

- **Say:** Today begins the season of Advent. *(Write the word* Advent *on the board.)* Advent is a time when we get ready for Christmas by thinking again about the Christmas story! For the next few weeks as we get ready for Christmas, we will learn all we can about Joseph.

- **Say:** Who knows who Joseph was? *(Allow responses.)* Yes, Joseph was the earthly father of Jesus. We'll find out today that Joseph's plan for his life did not turn out exactly as he thought it would. Joseph was not planning to be the father of Jesus, but Joseph wanted to do what God asked him to. He followed God's plan. Joseph put God's plan ahead of his own plans. More on that to come.

Large Group

Bring all the children together for some activities. Use a bell to alert the children to the large group time.

Humble Word Discovery

- Create teams of six players each. Arrange each team in line behind one of the starting lines.

- Mix up each set of letters for the word HUMBLE. About 12-15 feet away from each starting line, place a set of mixed-up letters face-down on the floor or a table. (Don't tell the children the word.)

- Give the first person in line for each team an inflated balloon.

- **Say:** When I say "Go," the first person in line gently bats the balloon down to the pile of letters without letting the balloon touch the ground. When you get to the letters, pick up one letter and then bat the balloon back down to where you started while carrying the letter you selected. Then hand the balloon off to the next person in line and stand facing your team with your letter showing. As each new letter is brought back, team members should try to figure out the word and unscramble it. Play continues until all six letters have been chosen and the word has been revealed and unscrambled. First team to display the word spelled correctly wins!!

- **Notes:** Make the game extra fun by playing some music. If you have mostly younger children playing, don't scramble the letters, and have an adult or older leader help them spell the word correctly. If any children are not playing, keep them involved by having them cheer for one of the teams.

- At the end of the game, ask the children what word they spelled. *(Allow responses.)*

- **Say:** Can anyone tell me what the word *humble* means? *(Allow responses.)* For today, we are going to say that being humble means we are putting others first ahead of ourselves.

- **Say:** Today, as we begin the Christmas story we are going to see that Joseph was incredibly humble. Part of me wonders if this is why God asked Joseph to be Jesus' earthly father—because of how humble Joseph was. Now let's learn a little bit more about Joseph.

Prepare

- ✓ Supplies needed: paper, marker, balloons, tape; optional: music player

- ✓ Print out the letters of the word HUMBLE, all caps, one letter per sheet, taking up the entire sheet (one set of letters per team of six).

- ✓ Use masking tape to mark off a starting line (one starting line per team of six, with lines arranged next to one another).

- ✓ Inflate enough balloons that each team will have one, plus one or two extra (in case of accidental popping).

Prepare

✓ Supplies needed: watch, clock, or timer; whiteboard or large sheet of paper; something to write with

Bible Story Experience

- Gather the children around you and have a whiteboard or large sheet of paper that you can write on. Instruct someone to watch the time for one minute.

- **Say:** When I say "Go," I want you to yell out all the different jobs you can have as an adult. For example, you might say teacher. As you yell out the jobs, I'll write them down. We'll do this for one minute. Are you ready? Go!

- Write quickly as the children yell out jobs. If they need more ideas, feel free to help.

- At the end of one minute, call time and thank the children for all the great ideas. Now look at the list and read it back to the children. Then ask the children to name what jobs they think are the coolest. See if you can come up with a top-three list. (Don't spend too much time on this.)

- Carpenter may or may not make the overall list. If it does, it probably will not make the top-three list. If it's not on the lists, that is totally fine and may help with the point of this experience.

- **Say:** What was Joseph's job in the Bible? *(carpenter)* Probably not one of the coolest jobs in the world, right? But we do know that Joseph worked hard, as most carpenters do. Carpenters work long hours to build things out of wood. Joseph probably made handles for tools and other furniture pieces. I wonder if Joseph liked being a carpenter? *(Allow responses.)* A carpenter must make things just right for people and put what they need first. That again shows us Joseph's humility.

- **Say:** Joseph probably had some big plans for his life. Maybe he wanted to expand his business and build big furniture pieces. But God had other plans for Joseph. When God told Joseph the plans, Joseph said yes to God and no to his own plans. That is what it means to be humble. So, there are two examples of Joseph being humble. Now I'll show you a few more examples of humility.

Pictures of Jesus' Humility

- Gather the children around you. Show them, in turn, each of the pictures you drew before the session. Discuss the pictures with them.

  o (Picture #1) **Say:** Jesus was sometimes interrupted by the crowds. Often he had plans to be somewhere and to do something but people wanted to hear Jesus preach and help their illnesses. Jesus always put the crowds first. Who was Jesus putting first in these situations? Himself or others? *(Allow responses.)* Jesus was being humble!

  o (Picture #2) **Say:** Jesus hung out with a tax collector and had dinner with him. Everyone laughed at Jesus and couldn't believe he was hanging out with this guy. Who was Jesus putting first then? Himself or the tax collector? *(Allow responses.)* Jesus was being humble!

  o (Picture #3) **Say:** Jesus was born in a manger, a trough that animals ate out of. Jesus left heaven, the coolest place, and was born in a trough, because he loves you and me. Who was Jesus putting first? Himself or others? *(Allow responses.)* Jesus was being humble!

  o (Picture #4) **Say:** Jesus died on a cross to take away the sins and bad stuff that we've done. Jesus never did anything wrong, and yet he took the punishment for all our bad stuff. Who was Jesus putting first then? Himself or others? *(Allow responses.)* Jesus was being humble!

- **Say:** I wonder if, as Jesus was growing up, Joseph was the one who taught him about being humble and putting others first. What do you think? *(Allow responses,)*

- **Say:** Let's open our Bibles to Philippians 2:3 and listen to these words: "Don't do anything for selfish purposes, but with humility think of others as better than yourselves."

- **Say:** When we are humble and begin putting others first ahead of ourselves, we are being more like Jesus and Joseph. In some ways the Christmas story really begins with Joseph, who put Jesus first ahead of his own plans. Let's pray before breaking into groups. *(You can pray or ask one of the children to say a prayer.)*

Prepare

✓ Supplies needed: posterboard, markers

✓ Sketch the following four pictures of Jesus that show times when he was humble. (You don't have to be a good artist; in fact, I've found when I draw lame stick figures the children enjoy them just as much!)

✓ Picture #1: Draw Jesus in a crowd of people. Have the crowd asking Jesus questions.

✓ Picture #2: Draw Jesus with Zacchaeus. Maybe Zacchaeus is in a tree or carrying some money bags. Have people around the picture with unhappy faces.

✓ Picture #3: Draw a Christmas scene with Jesus in a manger with parents and animals around.

✓ Picture #4: Draw a cross.

Small Groups

Divide the children into small groups. You may organize the groups around age levels or around readers and nonreaders. Keep the groups small, with a maximum of ten children in each group. You may need to have more than one group of each age level.

Prepare

✓ Supplies needed: signs that say *Yes* and *No*, tape, whiteboard or large sheet of paper, markers, craft sticks (wide ones will work best)

✓ Tape the *Yes* sign on one side of the room and the *No* sign on the other side of the room.

Younger Children (Grades K–2)

- **Say:** Today we've been talking about Joseph the earthly father of Jesus and how humble he was. We know that being humble means putting others first.

- **Say:** I'm going to read you a few stories. At the end of each story I want to know if you think the people in the story are humble. If you think they are humble, stand near the *Yes* sign. If you think they are not humble, stand near the *No* sign. Are you ready? *(If you or the children want to make up more stories, you can use those too.)*

  o Story #1: The teacher says it's time for recess. Avery loves recess and runs to the front of the line to be the first one outside. On her way to the front of the line, Avery bumps into Jackson. Was Avery humble?

  o Story #2: Tyler's mom made delicious cookies for an after-school snack. There is one cookie left. Tyler's mom says Tyler can have it and that his little sister Lily can have something else. Tyler decides to split the cookie in half with his little sister. Was Tyler humble?

  o Story #3: Lauren has invited her friend Alison over to play Candyland. Alison plays Candyland all the time at home and doesn't want to play it today. Lauren doesn't listen to Alison and makes her play Candyland anyway. Was Lauren humble?

  o Story #4: Chase's church is collecting money for some kids who won't be getting any Christmas presents this year. Chase has been saving his money for three weeks to buy a super-cool toy at the store. When he hears about this collection, Chase gives half his money to help these kids have a great Christmas. Was Chase humble?

  o Story #5: Rose spends the entire afternoon playing with her younger brother and watching all his favorite TV shows, even the ones she has seen over and over again! Was Rose humble?

- **Say:** Sometimes it's easy to be humble, and sometimes it's hard. Why do you think Jesus wants us to be humble? *(Allow responses.)*

Take It Home

- **Say:** As we wrap up our lesson about being humble, let's create a reminder that we can take home with us to put others first.

- Write the word *humble* on a whiteboard or large sheet of paper for the kids to see.

- Hand each child a craft stick.

- Allow time for them to decorate one side of the popsicle stick with a marker and on the other side write and decorate the word *humble*.

- **Say:** Let's pray before ending our session:

  Dear Lord, thank you for Christmas! Thank you for the story of Joseph, who put others first before himself. Joseph was humble. Jesus, you are also humble. Help us all to be humble and put others first before ourselves. In Jesus' name. Amen!

✓ Supplies needed: signs numbered 1-10; tape, notecards, markers

✓ Tape the numbered signs around the room to create stations where children can stand

Older Children (Grades 3-6)

- **Say:** I'm going to read you some stories in which people show humility by putting others first. As you hear each story, move to a number around the room that shows how hard you think it was for that person to show humility. If you think it was easy, move to a lower number; if you think it was hard, move to a higher number. Ready? (*If you or the children want to make up more stories, you can use those too.*)

  o Story #1: Lauren has invited a friend over to her house because she really wants to play her new video game with her. Her friend Alison plays this game all the time at home and doesn't want to play it today. Lauren is disappointed but allows Alison to choose what she wants to do instead. How hard was it for Lauren to be humble in this story?

  o Story #2: Chase's church is collecting money for some kids who will not be getting Christmas presents this year. Chase has been saving his money for three weeks to buy a super-cool toy at the store. When he hears about this collection, Chase gives half his money to help these kids have a great Christmas. How hard was it for Chase to be humble?

  o Story #3: Rose's younger brother always begs Rose to play with him. Rose decides to spend the next hour playing with her younger brother and watching his favorite TV shows, even the ones she has seen over and over again. Rose really wanted to do something else but hangs with her brother instead. How hard was it for Rose to be humble?

  o Story #4: Grandma and Grandpa are coming over to Jackson's house and have offered to take either Jackson or his brother Will to the movies. They have decided to take one person at a time on a special adventure every month. There is a great movie out that Jackson wants to see, but Jackson allows his brother Will to go first with their grandparents. How hard was it for Jackson to be humble?

  o Story #5: At recess, teams are being chosen for a kickball game. Alex gets to pick players for his team. He knows who the best players are, but instead of choosing them he selects a couple of kids who never get picked. How hard was it for Alex to be humble?

- Gather your group together and talk about these questions:
  o When is it hardest to be humble? Is it ever easy to be humble?

  o Why do you think putting others first is important to Jesus?

  o How can you remember to be humble this week?

Faithful: Children's Leader Guide

Take It Home

- Hand out notecards and markers to your group.

- **Say:** Sometimes we need reminders to be humble and put others first. So for the next few minutes you are going to create a "humble" card that you will take home. We want you to put it someplace where you will see it every day as a reminder to be humble.

- Instruct the children to write on one side of the card: "I will be humble by…"

- Have them turn the card over and on the other side write or draw a picture of how they will be humble.

- Then allow them time to decorate their cards however they wish.

- **Say:** Let's pray before ending our session:

  Dear Lord, thank you for Christmas! Thank you for the story of Joseph, who put others first before himself. Joseph was humble. Jesus, you are also humble. Help us all to be humble and put others first before ourselves. In Jesus' name. Amen!

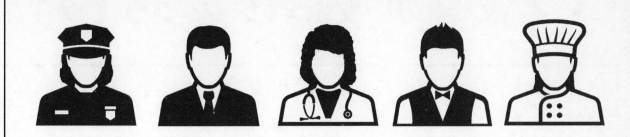

When I Grow Up!

When I grow up, I want to be a _____.

If I get to be a _____, I'll spend my days _____
_____.

The reason I'd love to be a _____ is _____
_____.

Here is a picture of me as a _____!

2 Joseph Trusts God's Plan

Objectives

The children will:

- Learn what it means to trust God
- Learn that Joseph trusted God
- Be ready to trust God when tough situations come up
- Learn that prayer is a first step toward trusting God more

Bible Story

Joseph Has a Visitor
Matthew 1:18-24

Bible Verse

Trust in the LORD with all your heart; don't rely on your own intelligence.

(Proverbs 3:5)

Focus for the Teacher

Ever had a day that didn't go according to plan? I'm sure that you, as a leader of children, have had that happen a time or two. I remember a road trip my wife and I took to visit family. We had the trip all planned out, from what day we were leaving to where we would stay during our trip. Everything was covered. As we were driving, the car began to smoke and eventually died along the side of the road. After getting towed to the nearest mechanic, we ended up sleeping in the car that night and spending a day waiting for it to be repaired. We then resumed our trip, which ended up looking nothing like we had planned.

We've all had days like that. Many of us have had plans that didn't just change a vacation but altered our lives, which brings us to Joseph. Joseph was a carpenter in Nazareth who was engaged to a young woman named Mary. I'm sure Joseph and Mary had plans for their engagement, wedding, and eventual life

> Trusting God isn't always easy.

together, but it all changed in the blink of an eye when Joseph learned that his wife would be having a baby who was the son of God, the long-awaited Messiah. Forget about questions of the virgin birth (this is a children's book) and instead just imagine how Joseph must have felt. He was going to be directly involved in God's plan to save the world!

Like anyone put into that situation, Joseph was initially unsure of what to do. He devised a plan to quietly take himself out of the picture, but God was persistent, and Joseph's faith allowed him to follow God's plan. The amount of trust Joseph showed during this situation was amazing! Wouldn't it be great if all of us could have that kind of faith? In session 2 of our study, we'll look at Joseph as a model for increasing our faith to help us all trust God. And by the way, if you didn't already know it, trusting God can be hard work!

Explore Interest Groups

Be sure that adult leaders are waiting when the first child arrives. Greet and welcome each child. Get the children involved in an activity that interests them and introduces the theme for the day's activities.

My Plans!

- As the children arrive, greet them by name and hand them a copy of **Reproducible 2a: My Plans!** Ask them to fill in the blanks or draw pictures to describe their plans for tomorrow. The plans can be real or imagined.

- Allow them 5-7 minutes to complete this task. Be sure to give them a two-minute warning and a one-minute warning before their time is up.

- Once time is called, bring the children together and allow some time for sharing. First, go around and find out their plans for tomorrow.

- After 2-3 minutes of sharing, ask these questions:
  - o On a scale of 1-10, how excited are you about your plans? (1 is not excited, and 10 is super excited.)
  - o On a scale of 1-10, how disappointed would you be if these plans did not work out? (1 is not disappointed, and 10 is super disappointed.)
  - o Has any of you ever had a day that didn't go the way you planned it? How did you feel?

- **Say:** In our story today, Joseph's plans are changed—not just plans for tomorrow but plans for the rest of his life! He learns that his soon-to-be wife Mary is going to give birth to Jesus. This makes Joseph nervous because he is not even married to Mary, and he wasn't planning on being the dad of Jesus! Can you imagine being Jesus' mom or dad? But we will find out in our story that Joseph trusts God's plan and decides to stick with Mary and Jesus.

Prepare

✓ Supplies needed: markers or crayons

✓ Go to **Reproducible 2a: My Plans!** at the end of this session and make enough copies for everyone in the group to have one.

Prepare

✓ Supplies needed: play dough, google eyes, pipe cleaners, and any other random craft supplies you have lying around

✓ Spread out these supplies on a table for children to select and use.

Crazy Dreams

- As the children arrive, greet them by name and show them the table of craft supplies. Tell them to think about a weird or funny dream they've had. (Depending on the age of your group, you may need to present some guidelines on what the dreams can be about.)

- Using the supplies available, ask children to create a prop or props that will help them describe their dream to others. Give them 5-7 minutes to complete the activity. Be sure to give two-minute and one-minute warnings as time winds down.

- Once time is called, have children partner up with one or two other children and share their dreams using the props they have made. Allow 2-3 minutes per person.

- See if you can pick out a couple of really weird dreams to share with the group.

- After sharing time is over, discuss these questions:
  o How many of you have dreams every night?
  o When you wake up after a dream, how do you feel?
  o Has anyone here ever had an angel appear in your dreams?

- **Say:** In our story today, Joseph has a weird but important dream. In Joseph's dream, an angel talks to him. The angel tells Joseph to stick with Mary, because she is going to be the mother of Jesus. After waking up from his dream, Joseph decides to trust God's plan. Because Joseph trusts God, he gets to be part of something amazing!

Large Group

Bring all the children together to experience the Bible story. Use a bell to alert the children to the large group time.

Trust the Boss!

- **Say:** In our story, Joseph decides to trust God's plan even though he doesn't know what will happen. We are going to play a game in which you will have to trust people on your team because you don't know what will happen.

- Divide your children into groups of 3-5. (Groups can be smaller or larger and still work.)

- Hand each group a stack of cups and a stack of notecards. Hold in your hands the copies of **Reproducible 2b: Cup Tower Pictures**.

- **Say:** I have in my hands pictures of cup towers that your team can choose to build. Some of the towers in the pictures are easy and some are harder. The trick is that only one person from each team can see the pictures and choose which one your team will build. This person will be the boss of the construction project and will tell the team how to build the project. Your team will have to trust your boss's directions, because the boss is the only one allowed to see the picture.

- Invite each group to select a boss. Pull all the bosses aside and give each of them a copy of the cup tower pictures. Give them a moment to look at the pictures and pick the tower their team will build.

- Remind them that the boss's job is to give the team directions for building the tower they have chosen, without showing the picture or touching the cups and notecards.

- When the bosses are back with their groups, tell the teams to raise their hands when they are finished. Allow enough time so most groups finish.

- If time permits, play one or more additional rounds, with the same groups but different bosses. Finish the game while interest is still high. Don't drag it out too long.

- *Notes:* If your children are younger, you may want to have older children or even leaders be the boss until the children get the hang of it. Also, we have provided cup tower plans for you, but feel free to create your own.

Prepare

✓ Supplies needed: lots of red plastic cups, 3x5 notecards, whiteboard or large sheet of paper, marker to write with

✓ Go to **Reproducible 2b: Cup Tower Pictures** at the end of this session and make enough copies so that when you divide your class into teams of 3-5 children, each team can have a copy.

- When the game is over, bring everyone together and ask the following questions:
  - o Which did you like better—being the boss or the builder? Why?
  - o What would have happened in your group if they had not believed what the boss was telling them?
  - o Was it easy or hard to trust the boss's directions?

- **Say:** Today we want to think about the word *trust*. *(Write the word on a whiteboard or large sheet of paper.)* All of you just had to trust the boss in our game. Can anyone tell me what the word *trust* means? *(Allow responses.)* Great ideas! *(You can either use your favorite definition from the kids or use this one: "A belief in the truth of a person or thing.")*

- **Say:** We trust a lot of things. We trust that the chair we sit in will hold us up. We trust that a bridge will get us across a river. We also trust people. We trust our parents when they tell us not to touch a stove because it's hot. We trust our coaches when they tell us to practice a certain way to make us better at a sport. And finally, we trust God because God loves us a whole bunch. We are now going to look at the story of Joseph and see how Joseph trusted God.

Small Groups

Divide the children into small groups. You may organize the groups around age levels or around readers and nonreaders. Keep the groups small, with a maximum of ten children in each group. You may need to have more than one group of each age level.

Young Children (Grades K-2)

Dear God, thank you for always being with me! Help me to trust you as Joseph did and to always do what's right. In Jesus' name. Amen.

- Begin by reading this Bible verse: "When Joseph woke up, he did just as an angel from God commanded and took Mary as his wife" (Matthew 1:24).

- **Say:** This verse shows the trust Joseph had in God's plan. Now let's look at one more Bible verse: "Trust in the LORD with all your heart; / don't rely on your own intelligence" (Proverbs 3:5).

- **Say:** Even though Joseph didn't understand God's plan, he still followed God and stuck by Mary. In Proverbs, the Bible tells us to trust God with all our heart, and don't just rely on what we know. That may sound hard, but it doesn't have to be. This coming week we'll work on one way we can trust God more, and that's by using prayer. This week, whenever you feel afraid, nervous, or unsure of yourself—or if you just want to remember that God is with you—I want you to stop and say a short prayer. What should you pray? Well, our final activity will tell you what you can say.

- Hand each child a half sheet of colored construction paper or cardstock.

- Hand out a prayer guide (the strip of paper containing the prayer) to each child and read it to the group.

- Show the children the art supplies and direct them to glue the prayer onto the paper. The children can decorate as they wish.

- When most of the group has finished the project, bring them back together.

- **Say:** It's easier to trust God if we remember that God is always around. We can talk to God anytime. God can give us the strength to do what's right and help us when we aren't sure what to do. I want you to take your decorated prayer home and put it somewhere you will see it every day. I want you to say the prayer every day this week, knowing that God is with you and you can trust God all the time. You may want to have a parent or family member help you read the prayer and recite it.

- Close the session in prayer. You can offer your own prayer, you can read the prayer below, or you can have a child say a prayer.

Dear God, help me to be more like Joseph and trust you. Thank you for always being with me and always keeping your promises. Thank you for Christmas and your son, Jesus. In Jesus' name. Amen!

Prepare

✓ Supplies needed: Bible, half sheets of colored construction paper or cardstock (one per child), markers, crayons, glue; optional: decorating items

✓ Create a prayer guide handout for each child by using the prayer shown at the bottom of the page. Type and print out multiple copies of the prayer, then cut the copies apart to make small strips of paper that will fit easily onto the half sheets of colored construction paper or cardstock.

Prepare

✓ Supplies needed: Bibles, blank paper, colored pencils or crayons, word cloud sample

Older Children (Grades 3-6)

- Begin by opening the Bible together and reading Matthew 1:18-24. You can read the Scripture or ask for volunteers, but don't force anyone to read out loud.

- After reading the Scripture discuss these questions:
  - o How do you think Joseph felt when he learned Mary was pregnant?
  - o List some things that probably changed for Joseph once he trusted God's plans.
  - o How will you know what God's plans are for you?

- Next read or ask a volunteer to read Proverbs 3:5: "Trust in the LORD with all your heart; / don't rely on your own intelligence."

- After reading the Scripture discuss these questions:
  - o If someone asked you what it means to trust God, what would you say?
  - o Why is it hard sometimes to trust God?

- **Say:** Trusting God means trying to follow God and the teachings of Jesus in the Bible. It means when we need help we first go to Jesus in prayer. It means we do the right thing even when it doesn't make sense. It means we remember that God is always with us even when things are hard. Trusting God can mean all this and lots more.

- Hand out a blank sheet of paper and colored pencils or crayons to each child.

- **Say:** How many of you know what a "word cloud" is? *(Show sample.)* We are going to take 5-7 minutes to create our own word clouds about what it means to trust God. The phrase "Trust God" will be front and center and the largest element of your word cloud. Then all around that phrase you'll add your own words in various sizes, telling what it means to you to trust God. Remember, the more important words should be bigger, and the less important words should be smaller.

- **Say:** Here are some examples of words you might include:
  - o Trust
  - o Joseph
  - o God's plans
  - o Doing the right thing
  - o Faith
  - o Believe
  - o Rely
  - o God is here!

- Give the children time to work on their word clouds. As your time draws to a close, encourage the children to show their word clouds to one another.

- **Say:** Be sure to take these word clouds home tonight and put them somewhere you will see them every day for the next week as a reminder to trust God, just as Joseph did.

- Close in prayer. You can pray, you can ask a child to pray, or you can read the prayer below.

  Dear God, thank you for Joseph, who put your plan in front of his own plans even when the plan didn't make sense to him. Help us this week to trust you when we are scared, confused, or need strength to do the right thing. Thank you for Christmas and your son, Jesus. Amen!

My Plans!

This is what time I will get up tomorrow: _____
_____

This is what I will eat tomorrow: _____
_____

Most of my day I will do this: _____
_____

I will play this app tomorrow: _____
_____

I will spend a lot of time with this person tomorrow: _____
_____

I will go to bed at this time tomorrow: _____
_____

Cup Tower Pictures

3 The Courage of Joseph

Objectives

The children will:

- Learn about the road trip Joseph and Mary took
- Learn about courage and how to get it

Bible Story

The Birth of Jesus
Luke 2:1-7

Bible Verse

I've commanded you to be brave and strong, haven't I? Don't be alarmed or terrified, because the LORD your God is with you wherever you go.

(Joshua 1:9)

Focus for the Teacher

My wife and I have always enjoyed taking road trips. We began doing weekend road trips when we first got married, and since having kids we have continued to do road trips as a family. Our road trips have ranged from short three-hour drives over a weekend to long twenty-hour drives to visit family and friends in New England. (We live in Kansas City.) For me, the best part of road trips is finding unusual places to stop and check out. Just recently on one of these road trips, our family found an exit to a town that laid claim to owning the world's largest rocking chair. Intrigued, we stopped and found not only a giant rocking chair but also the world's largest wind chimes, pencil, and mailbox. It was quite something and a memory our family still talks about on a regular basis.

Today, as we continue to see the story of Christmas through the eyes of Joseph, we'll look at Joseph and Mary's road trip from Nazareth to Bethlehem. As you may know, the Roman Empire announced a census that required everyone to head to their hometown to be registered. Mary was very pregnant, but she and Joseph made a difficult road trip, traveling eight-

> Have courage to follow God.

plus miles over a span of a few days to arrive in Bethlehem.

Since I'm a guy, I've never experienced being pregnant, so I can't imagine what it was like for Mary to travel in her condition. But I do wonder what was going through Joseph's mind when the census was announced. Since we are looking at Joseph this Advent season, we'll reflect on his feelings and thoughts as he prepared and then took part in a road trip like none other.

Joseph had already signed on to be part of God's amazing story in bringing Jesus to earth, but, learning about the census and road trip, he must have wondered what was going on and why. In spite of any doubts he may have had, Joseph continued his commitment to Mary and to God and courageously walked by Mary's side all the way to Bethlehem, where the son of God would be born. For Joseph and for us, following God's plan is not always easy; it takes courage. In this lesson we'll look for courage to follow God.

Explore Interest Groups

Be sure that adult leaders are waiting when the first child arrives. Greet and welcome each child. Get the children involved in an activity that interests them and introduces the theme for the day's activities.

Create Your Own Road Trip!

- As the children arrive, hand each of them a piece of paper and something to write and draw with. Tell them they can create a road trip to anywhere in the United States; money is no problem.

- To help them plan their trip, have them answer the following five questions by either writing or drawing their answers on their sheet of paper.

    o   Where are you going?

    o   What are you riding? (car, train, horse, bike, and so forth)

    o   What snacks will you bring?

    o   Where will you stay as you travel?

    o   What games, books, movies, and other things will you bring to keep you entertained on the trip?

- After the children have answered the questions, tell them to turn over the paper and draw a map showing their road trip and the route they will take. Allow them to be creative on this! They can refer to maps that you have brought, or they may want to create a map from memory or even an imaginary map.

- After the children have had a few minutes to work, call time. (Be sure to give them a two-minute and a one-minute warning.) Allow a few children to share if they would like to do so.

- **Say:** Raise your hand if you enjoy going on a road trip! Road trips can be fun! In our story for today, we'll see that Joseph is going on a road trip with Mary, who is about to give birth to the baby Jesus. Their road trip was not planned, and in fact it was probably a trip they didn't want to take. They were traveling about seventy miles from Nazareth to Bethlehem and would be walking most of the way. (Mary may have had a donkey to ride on.) Does anyone know why Joseph and Mary had to go to Bethlehem? *(Allow responses.)* Yes, that's right. They had to be counted by the government. We'll see that the trip was probably very hard and required a lot of courage.

Prepare

✓ Supplies needed: paper, pencils, markers, crayons, some maps for the children to refer to if needed

✓ Before the session, you may want to write and display the five questions listed at the left.

Prepare

✓ Supplies needed: United States map, pencils

✓ Go to **Reproducible 3a: How Far Is That?** at the end of this session and make enough copies for everyone in the group to have one.

✓ Before the session, display the US map where all the children can see it.

How Far Is That?

- As the children arrive, show them the US map that you've displayed. Then pass out to each child a pencil and a copy of **Reproducible 3a: How Far Is That?**

- **Say:** We're going to guess how long it would take to walk between some cities in the United States. On your sheet you'll see ten pairs of cities, and below each pair you'll see two choices, *a* and *b*, saying roughly how long it could take to walk between the cities. Your job is to look at the cities, check the map, and decide which answer is correct, *a* or *b*. Circle it with your pencil. No cell phones can be used during this activity!

- Give them a few minutes to circle their answers, then read the correct answers (1b, 2b, 3a, 4b, 5a, 6a, 7b, 8a, 9a, 10b). Children can keep track of how many answers they get right.

- **Say:** Today our story of Joseph moves to a long road trip that Joseph and Mary had to take. They walked seventy miles from Nazareth to Bethlehem. The walk took extra long because Mary was pregnant and about to give birth to Jesus. It probably took them a few days to complete because Mary was pregnant. (Mary may have had a donkey to ride on.) Does anyone know why Joseph and Mary had to go to Bethlehem? *(Allow responses)* Yes, that's right. They had to be counted by the government. We'll see that the trip was probably very hard and required a lot of courage.

- If you know someone in your church who is pregnant it might be fun to have her come to your group and talk for a few minutes about how hard it is to move around when you are pregnant. Ask her if she could imagine walking seventy miles while pregnant.

Large Group

Bring all the children together for some activities. Use a bell to alert the children to the large group time.

Copycats

- Gather the group together.

- **Ask:** How many of you have ever copycatted someone before? This is when you say and do exactly what the other person (such as an older brother or sister) says and does. Usually it's pretty annoying, right? Well, for the next few minutes you're going to copycat me, and I'm going to like it!

- **Say:** Here's how to play. When I say, "ice cream," everyone will stand up and begin copying everything I say and do. When I say, "pizza," everyone will sit down and stop copying me. Let's practice first.

  o Ice cream! *(They stand up and start copying.)*
  o Hello *(Wave.)*
  o I love Christmas. *(Point to your heart.)*
  o You are sooo cool! *(Make thumbs up.)*
  o Pizza! *(They sit down and stop copying.)*
  o Great job! *(Make double thumbs up—but they don't copy.)*

- **Say:** You guys are good. Okay, ready for the real thing? Here we go!

  o Ice cream! *(They stand up and start copying.)*
  o Joseph and Mary were worried. *(Make a worried face.)*
  o Mary was very pregnant. *(Rub your belly.)*
  o With baby Jesus. *(Rock arms, then point to sky.)*
  o Joseph had to go to Bethlehem, and it was a long trip. *(Point into the distance.)*
  o Like, seventy miles. *(Hold up seven fingers, ten times.)*
  o It was tax time. *(Rub fingers together in the sign for money.)*
  o Joseph couldn't say no to the trip. *(Shake head no.)*
  o What to do, what to do? *(Make a confused face and scratch head.)*
  o Finally, he decided to trust God! *(Point to sky.)*

  o Pizza! *(They sit down and stop copying.)*
  o It would take courage. *(Pose like a superhero with hands on hips.)*
  o There was no car. *(Move hands in the air pretending to steer.)*
  o They had to walk. *(Walk in place.)*
  o They did have a donkey for Mary to ride. *(Make a donkey sound.)*
  o They said goodbye to their friends. *(Wave goodbye.)*
  o And began walking. *(Walk in place.)*

Prepare

- ✓ Copycats is a game based on the annoying tradition of a younger sibling copying everything an older sibling does and says. Today you'll use this tradition to your advantage as you retell the story of Joseph and Mary's journey to Bethlehem.

- ✓ The script (see left) consists of a series of short, concise sentences, each followed by a motion in parentheses. Be sure to read it over a few times before the session, as the more familiar you are with the script, the better this experience will go.

o   Ice cream! (*They stand up and start copying.*)

o   They walked some more. (*Walk in place.*)

o   It took over a week—like, eight days. (*Hold up eight fingers.*)

o   When they arrived, they were so happy. (*Jump in the air.*)

o   But Mary was still pregnant. (*Rub belly.*)

o   And baby Jesus was about to be born. (*Pretend to rock a baby.*)

o   But their trip had been safe. (*Make "OK" sign.*)

o   Because Joseph had courage. (*Pose like a superhero with hands on hips.*)

o   And trusted God. (*Point to sky.*)

o   But what would happen next? (*Shrug shoulders, palms up.*)

o   Pizza! (*Game ends.*)

Prepare

✓ Supplies needed: a timer, suitcases (one for each team of five), road-trip items (clothes, snacks, water bottle, soap, travel games, phone charger, pillow, and so forth)

✓ Place the suitcases, one per team, at the far end of the room. At the near end, place the road-trip items in piles, one pile per team, with an equal number of items in each pile. (A pile of five or ten items would be fine.)

Packing for a Trip

• Divide your group into teams of five or fewer, each having an equal number of players. Have each team stand next to a pile of road-trip items.

• **Say:** When I say go, the first person in line should grab one item from your team pile, race to your team's suitcase, open it, and put the item inside. Then race back to your team and tag the next person in line, who does the same thing.

• Play continues until the road-trip items are all gone. Then the next person in lines races down, closes the suitcase, and carries it back to her or his team. The first team that gets their suitcase back to the group wins!

• *Notes*: If you only have enough children for one team, you can time them for several races and compare the times. If running is not a possibility, spread each team out between the pile of travel items and the suitcase, then have them pass the items down the line. The last person in line then packs the suitcase for the group.

• After the game, bring your group back together and ask the following questions:

o   What is the one thing you always want to take when you go on a road trip?

o   Have you ever been surprised by a road trip and had to pack quickly?

o   How do you think Mary and Joseph were feeling about their road trip to Bethlehem? What things do you think they took?

Small Groups

Divide the children into small groups. You may organize the groups around age levels or around readers and nonreaders. Keep the groups small, with a maximum of ten children in each group. You may need to have more than one group of each age level.

Younger Children (Grades K-2)

- Have the children sit in a circle. Read Joshua 1:9 together as a group three times, in three different ways: first, in a loud voice; second, in a whispering voice; and third, in a squeaky voice like Mickey Mouse.

  o "I've commanded you to be brave and strong, haven't I? Don't be alarmed or terrified, because the LORD your God is with you wherever you go."

- **Ask:**

  o What does it mean to have courage?

  o Did Joseph have courage? Why or why not?

  o Do you know anyone who has lots of courage?

- **Say:** When we know that God is with us, we can have courage. Courage helps us do the right thing even when no one else is doing it. Courage helps us through a bad day when we're feeling sad.

- **Say:** I often think of superheroes like Batman, Wonder Woman, and Superman—they have lots of courage, don't they? That's one of the things that makes them super! Today you're going to transform into superheroes by making capes. When you put on your cape, you'll remember that God is with you, and when you remember that, you'll have courage, the way Joseph did in the story.

- Hand each child a white trash bag and a marker or markers. Unfold the bag all the way, but don't open it up.

- **Say:** Here are your capes. Your job is to decorate your cape with markers, adding pictures and words that remind you to have courage because God is with you. *(Decoration examples: strong muscle arms, superhero images, word such as* Courage.*)* Encourage the children to be creative.

- Give them 5-7 minutes to work on their capes. Give them two-minute and one-minute warnings before calling time.

- As the children finish, take pieces of duct tape and fasten their capes to their shoulders. Be sure they are wearing sleeves; don't duct-tape skin! Packing tape and masking tape will work too.

- *Note:* Online you can find a fairly simple way to cut trash bags into capes so you don't need tape.

Prepare

- ✓ Supplies needed: Bible, white trash bags (one per child), markers, duct tape; optional: scissors

- ✓ Try writing on one of the trash bags with a marker and make sure to select one that doesn't smear.

- Once everyone is finished, have the children stand around the room in their best superhero poses. Admire and compliment their poses.

- **Say:** Repeat after me: God is always with me, *(Pause.)* so I can have courage. *(Pause.) (Repeat 3-4 times, speaking more loudly each time.)*

- Bring everyone together in a circle to wrap up.

- **Say:** We see in the Bible that Joseph needed courage that first Christmas. The Bible says that all of us can be strong and have courage because God is with us. But how do we remember that God is with us when we are at school, on a sports team, or at a music lesson? *(Allow responses.)*

- **Say:** One way we can remember that God is with us is by praying. Whenever we're in a situation and don't know what to do, we can stop and pray. It doesn't have to be a big, long, loud prayer. It can be a quick prayer in your head asking God to give you courage to do the right thing. Now let's close with prayer:

    Dear Lord, thank you for the courage of Joseph on that first Christmas. Help us to remember that you are always with us, and we don't have to be afraid because you give us strength and courage to make it through tough times. In Jesus' name. Amen.

Older Children (Grades 3-6)

- Bring the group together and open your Bible to Joshua 1:9. You can read it or ask a volunteer to read it. Read it twice so children really get a chance to hear the words.

  o "I've commanded you to be brave and strong, haven't I? Don't be alarmed or terrified, because the LORD your God is with you wherever you go."

- **Ask:**

  o How much courage did Joseph have, not just during the road trip but throughout the whole Christmas story? *(Allow responses.)*

  o Can you list any other Bible characters who had courage, or list people you know who you think have a lot of courage? *(Make a list on the board.)*

  o According to Joshua 1:9, why can we have courage? Where does courage come from? *(knowing that God is with us)*

- **Say:** We can have courage to do the right thing or to make it through hard times, because we know that God is with us. I think this is how Joseph made it through the first Christmas. He knew that God was with him every step of the way. Joseph was not alone.

- **Say:** Sometimes we forget that God is with us and gives us courage to do what's right and make it through hard times. So we're going to make posters to illustrate this idea: We can have courage because God is with us.

- Divide the children into groups of two or three people. Give each group one posterboard and a handful of markers.

- Tell the groups they are each going to make a poster to help them remember to have courage because God is with them.

- Encourage the groups to get creative with their posters. They could draw fun pictures illustrating a situation where courage is needed; show Joseph on the poster; illustrate a Christmas scene; or show only words that say, "Have courage! God is with you!"

- Give the groups 6-7 minutes to finish. Be sure to give two-minute and one-minute warnings.

- Afterward, have groups present their posters to the other children. Once all the groups have presented, congratulate them on a job well done.

- If your church allows it, hang the posters in the room or halls.

The Courage of Joseph

- **Say:** We see in the Bible that Joseph needed courage that first Christmas. The Bible says that all of us can be strong and have courage because God is with us. But how do we remember that God is with us when we are at school, on a sports team, or at a music lesson? *(Allow responses.)*

- **Say:** One way we can remember that God is with us is by praying. Whenever we're in a situation and don't know what to do, we can stop and pray. It doesn't have to be a big, long, loud prayer. It can be a quick prayer in your head asking God to give you courage to do the right thing. Now let's close with prayer:

  Dear Lord, thank you for the courage of Joseph on that first Christmas. Help us to remember that you are always with us, and we don't have to be afraid because you give us strength and courage to make it through tough times. In Jesus' name. Amen.

How Far Is That?

1. New York City to Los Angeles
a. 512 hours
b. 912 hours

2. Boston to Washington, DC
a. 97 hours
b. 147 hours

3. Philadelphia to Baltimore
a. 33 hours
b. 22 hours

4. Orlando to Atlanta
a. 175 hours
b. 146 hours

5. Dallas to Chicago
a. 310 hours
b. 275 hours

6. Kansas City, MO to Nashville
a. 184 hours
b. 105 hours

7. Salt Lake City to Phoenix
a. 300 hours
b. 200 hours

8. Cleveland to Detroit
a. 54 hours
b. 74 hours

9. Denver to Seattle
a. 435 hours
b. 505 hours

10. Houston to Juneau, AK
a. 1140 hours
b. 1745 hours

4 Jesus Is Born! Joseph Celebrates!

Objectives

The children will:

- Learn about the climax of the Christmas story
- Celebrate the joy Jesus brings
- Share the joy!

Bible Story

The Shepherds
Luke 2:8-20

Bible Verse

The angel said, "Don't be afraid! Look! I bring good news to you—wonderful, joyous news for all people."
(Luke 2:10)

Focus for the Teacher

Ten years ago, my wife and I celebrated the birth of our triplet sons! Born seven weeks early, all three were in good health. After a high-risk pregnancy, we definitely celebrated. I can still remember as plain as day the first time my wife got to hold all three babies. (I had gotten first dibs, because she was still recovering from the birth. Not fair, I know!) Our joy and happiness were indescribable, and very few things since have compared to that moment. (The birth of our daughter might have counted, but she was born in a snowstorm, and I was just relieved that we made it to the hospital safely.)

As I think about the moment when I knew our triplets were going to be okay, I can't help wondering if Joseph experienced that same joy and relief when Jesus was born. Not only were all pregnancies high-risk in Bible times, but think of what Joseph had been through in the months leading up to the birth. First, he found out that Mary was pregnant and he was not the

> Celebrate that Jesus is born!

biological father. Second, he had a visit from an angel. Third, he and Mary had traveled seventy miles at the end of her pregnancy. And finally, when they arrived in Bethlehem Mary gave birth in a stable—the Bible equivalent of a parking garage. What a wild ride! Surely he felt joy and relief.

As we close in on Christmas, take a few moments to really celebrate and experience the joy that comes from knowing Jesus is here! I give you permission to enjoy an unhealthy snack in celebration of Jesus' arrival!

Explore Interest Groups

Be sure that adult leaders are waiting when the first child arrives. Greet and welcome each child. Get the children involved in an activity that interests them and introduces the theme for the day's activities.

Something to Consider

If it makes sense and you can prepare far enough in advance, consider making this time with your children a birthday party for Jesus. Purchase balloons and birthday decorations. Have some yummy snacks (ideally a birthday cake). Play games (provided in the lesson), and just celebrate.

Add meaning to the celebration by choosing a mission project that your children can participate in. Give them a week's notice to bring in gifts for Jesus. These gifts can be donated to whatever mission you have decided on. Ideas include: Toys for Tots, books for local elementary schools that have limited budgets, and canned food for homeless shelters. HAPPY BIRTHDAY, JESUS!

Birthday Party for Jesus

- Play some good party music as the children arrive. Encourage them to help decorate the area for a birthday party for Jesus.

- Some of the children can create a banner from the long sheet of paper, decorating it and writing their names on it.

- Other children may choose to create their own individual signs for the birthday boy.

- Once the banner and signs are finished, have the group tape them to the wall. Add balloons and other decorations if you want to.

- Once the room is decorated, bring the children together.

- **Say:** How many of you like birthday parties? What's your favorite thing about a birthday party? How many of you realize that Christmas is really a big birthday party for Jesus? Christmas, coming up very soon, is a celebration of when Jesus was born, and in some ways it's very much like a birthday party. I'm sure Joseph was celebrating that Jesus was born. Today, parts of our lesson will just be celebrating and having fun because Jesus was born. Christmas brings us hope, and it's a reminder that Jesus loves us so much that he came to earth and was born in a manger just for you and just for me!

Prepare

✓ Supplies needed: long sheet of paper, sheets of regular-sized colored paper, tape, markers, party music and appropriate player

✓ Optional supplies: balloons, streamers, other birthday decorations

Prepare

✓ Supplies needed: dance music and appropriate player, open space to dance

✓ Optional supplies: headphones or earplugs, blindfold

Freeze Dance!

- As the children arrive, play some great upbeat dance music. Bring the group together to play a game of Freeze Dance.

- While the music is playing, everyone is free dancing.

- When the music stops, everyone must freeze in a pose that the leader calls out.

- To add a twist to the game, invite one person to the front of the room and give the person a blindfold and headphones or earplugs to block sound. Have him or her turn away from the crowd until the group freezes. Then, when everyone else is frozen, the volunteer turns around and tries to guess what they're frozen as.

- Here are some ideas for what the children can freeze as:
  - o ninja
  - o robot
  - o Statue of Liberty
  - o sprinkler
  - o kangaroo
  - o rabbit
  - o skier
  - o runner
  - o tree
  - o star
  - o letters Y, M, C, A (one at a time)

- Once the game has been played for a while, bring everyone together.

- **Say:** How many of you like birthday parties? *(Allow responses.)* What is your favorite thing about a birthday party? *(Allow responses.)* How many of you realize that Christmas is really a big birthday party for Jesus? Christmas, which is coming up very soon, is a celebration of when Jesus was born, much like a birthday party. Today some parts of our lesson will just be celebrating and having fun because Jesus was born. I'm sure Joseph was celebrating that Jesus was born. I wonder if he danced! Christmas brings us hope, and it's a reminder that Jesus loves us so much that he came to earth and was born in a manger just for you and just for me!

My Awesome Party!

- Have the children stand in a circle.

- As the children arrive, ask them to think about their next birthday party. If they could do anything, invite anyone, and eat anything, what would they choose and what would their party look like?

- Hand each of them a copy of **Reproducible 4a: My Awesome Party**, which has some questions to help them think about it.

- Allow them to fill out the sheet by either writing or drawing their answers to the questions. Then, on the back, have them create an invitation or poster about their party.

- Give the children 5-7 minutes to complete the project. Don't forget to give them two-minute and one-minute warnings.

- Afterward, bring the children together and allow them to share what they decided their parties would look like. If you have a lot of kids who want to share, have them first share with a partner and then have just a few share with the whole group. (You should fill out a sheet too! The children would love to hear your plans for an awesome party.)

- **Say:** How many of you like birthday parties? *(Allow responses)* What is your favorite thing about a birthday party? *(Allow responses.)* How many of you realize that Christmas is really a big birthday party for Jesus? Christmas, which is coming up very soon, is a celebration of when Jesus was born, much like a birthday party. Today some parts of our lesson will just be celebrating and having fun because Jesus was born. I'm sure Joseph was celebrating that Jesus was born. I wonder if he danced! Christmas brings us hope, and it's a reminder that Jesus loves us so much that he came to earth and was born in a manger just for you and just for me!

Prepare
✓ Supplies needed: something to write with

✓ Go to **Reproducible 4a: My Awesome Party!** at the end of this session and make a copy for each person in the class.

Large Group

Bring all the children together for some activities. Use a bell to alert the children to the large group time.

Prepare

✓ Supplies needed: baby doll, male and female clothes, stuffed animals, random supplies that you choose (one set of these props per team)

Create Your Own Nativity Scene

- Divide your group into teams of 6-8 if possible. (It works better if you have at least two groups.)

- Provide each team with a baby doll, male and female clothes, stuffed animals, and other random supplies. These props don't have to be the same, but the one consistent item should be the baby doll.

- Give teams 3-5 minutes to create a Christmas Nativity scene, including all the props you gave them.

- Call time after five minutes. Be sure to give two-minute and one-minute warnings.

- Allow a spokesperson for each team to explain what they created.

- You may want to snap a picture of each Nativity scene to share with your families or on your church's social-media accounts.

- *Note*: Don't worry about getting lots of props. You can probably get by with just a baby doll for each group and then a few other random props, even if they don't have anything to do with the Christmas story. Kids are creative, and you'll be amazed at how they can work a bottle of ketchup into a Nativity scene.

- **Say:** Most of us know what took place that first Christmas. Jesus' bed was a manger (a trough that animals eat out of). There was no nice place for Mary and Joseph to stay, so they hung out with the animals.

- **Say:** We've been talking about Joseph these past few weeks. How do you think Joseph was feeling when Jesus was born? *(Allow responses.)* I'll bet Joseph was pretty excited that Jesus made it! Joseph had been through a lot since he found out Mary would be the mother of Jesus. To help us think about Joseph's excitement level let's think about things that have made you excited in your life.

Prepare

✓ Supplies needed: emoji signs to tape around the room

✓ Before class, print out or draw big emoji symbols (one per sheet of paper) representing a variety of excited feelings. Post these around the room with space in between.

How Excited Are You?

- Tell the children that you are going to read a few exciting things to them. When they hear each exciting thing, they should move next to the emoji sign that best describes how they would feel. (There are no right or wrong answers.)

  o Your teacher says there will be no more homework the rest of the school year!

  o The *[insert local sports team]* have just won the championship!

  o Tomorrow you are eating pizza for dinner!

o You just found twenty dollars in the parking lot!

o You are going to the beach for vacation!

o Your favorite TV show will be on all day tomorrow!

o You can have ice cream for breakfast!

o *[Insert a few of your own if time allows.]*

- **Say:** These are all pretty exciting things! But imagine how exciting it was to Joseph when Jesus was born. Mary and the baby were healthy and safe. Jesus the Son of God was here, and Joseph was one of the first people to meet him. Let's review the story of that first Christmas before we break into small groups.

Bible Story Experience

- **Say:** Earlier some of you came up with a list of rules.

- Show the children the posters.

- **Say:** What joy Joseph must have felt that first Christmas! I wonder how he felt as he looked around the manger and saw Mary holding Jesus. Then I wonder what he thought as the shepherds came to visit.

- **Say:** Let's think about the meaning of Christmas just a little bit more by looking at four symbols of Christmas. Can someone tell us what a symbol is? *(Allow responses.)* You'll see these four symbols everywhere.

- One by one, reveal each symbol of Christmas listed below.

  o **Christmas lights** *(Plug them in.)*: Jesus is the light of the world. At night, it is so awesome to see light shining in the darkness. Joseph knew that Jesus came as the one true light of the world!

  o **Bells:** The sound of jingle bells reminds us of the joy and happiness Joseph felt and we feel in knowing that Jesus came to earth for us!

  o **Gifts:** God's perfect present to Joseph, Mary, and all of us was Jesus. Do you think Joseph knew what a perfect gift Jesus was to everyone?

  o **Candy Cane:** Do you notice the candy cane's shape? It looks like the staff that a shepherd would use to guide his sheep. It also looks like the letter J, which stands for Jesus or Joseph!

- I hope that when you see these symbols, they will remind you about the true meaning of Christmas.

Prepare

✓ Supplies needed: Christmas lights, bells, gifts in boxes or bags, candy cane (a giant one if possible), plain bags or a blanket

✓ Hide the Christmas items in separate bags or cover them with a big blanket until it is time to reveal each one.

Small Groups

Divide the children into small groups. You may organize the groups around grade levels or around readers and nonreaders. Keep the groups small, with a maximum of ten children in each group. You may need to have more than one group at each grade level.

Prepare

✓ Supplies needed: red and green construction paper, markers, Christmas stickers, card-decorating materials

✓ If your church has a Christmas event or service coming up, the cards the children make can serve as invitations. Alternatively, the cards could become part of a mission project: find a local nursing home, school, or shelter where you can deliver the cards. If you want to use the cards in either way, find out guidelines and make arrangements with the appropriate people.

Younger Children (Grades K-2)

• **Say:** Today we've been talking about the joy and excitement that Joseph must have felt as he saw the baby Jesus for the first time. All of us experience that joy, knowing that Jesus loves us and came to earth for us. But we don't keep the joy to ourselves. We share it with others so they can feel the joy too!

• **Say:** Today we're going to make joy cards. These are cards you can give people to share the joy of Jesus.

• Give each child a sheet of construction paper, markers, stickers, and card-decorating materials.

• Have them fold the paper in half to make a card.

• Instruct them to decorate the front of the card and write on the inside of the card "Merry Christmas," "Jesus Is Born," or another Christmas phrase that expresses joy. (You may want to write these phrases on a whiteboard so younger children can copy them.)

• Invite the children to think of someone outside the church who would enjoy getting the card and sharing your Christmas joy. (You may want to help by supplying a list of the types of people or specific names.) Or explain to the children how you have arranged for the cards to be used.

• Allow time for the children to work and then bring your group together. Be sure to bless the cards before you leave. You can say a prayer, have a child pray, or read the prayer below.

Dear God, thank you for sending Jesus to this earth! Thank you for Christmas and the joy of Christmas. May these cards bring joy to others this Christmas season. In Jesus' name. Amen!

Faithful: Children's Leader Guide

Older Children (Grades 3-6)

- **Say:** Today we've been talking about the joy and excitement that Joseph must have felt as he saw the baby Jesus for the first time. All of us experience that joy, knowing that Jesus loves us and came to earth for us. But we don't keep the joy to ourselves. We share it with others so they can feel the joy too!

- **Say:** Today we will use the shape of a candy cane to help us share the joy of Christmas with those outside our church.

- Give each child paper or cardstock, markers, tape, scissors, and a candy cane.

- Instruct children to fold the paper in half to form a card.

- Have them decorate the cards. Tell them to leave a place to tape the candy cane to the front cover. (The candy cane will be added last, after the card is decorated.)

- As part of the decoration, have them write "Merry Christmas," "Jesus Is Born," or other Christmas phrases that express joy.

- Invite the children to think of someone outside the church who would enjoy getting the card and sharing your Christmas joy, or explain how you have arranged for the cards to be used.

- Allow time for the children to work and then bring your group together. Be sure to bless the cards before you leave. You can say a prayer, have a child pray, or read the prayer below.

Dear God, thank you for sending Jesus to this earth! Thank you for Christmas and the joy of Christmas. May these cards bring joy to others this Christmas season. In Jesus' name. Amen!

Prepare

✓ Supplies needed: candy canes, tape, scissors, markers, construction paper or cardstock (thicker paper will work best)

✓ If your church has a Christmas event or service coming up, the cards the children make can serve as invitations. Alternatively, the cards could become part of a mission project: find a local nursing home, school, or shelter where you can deliver the cards. If you want to use the cards in either way, find out guidelines and make arrangements with the appropriate people.

My Awesome Party!

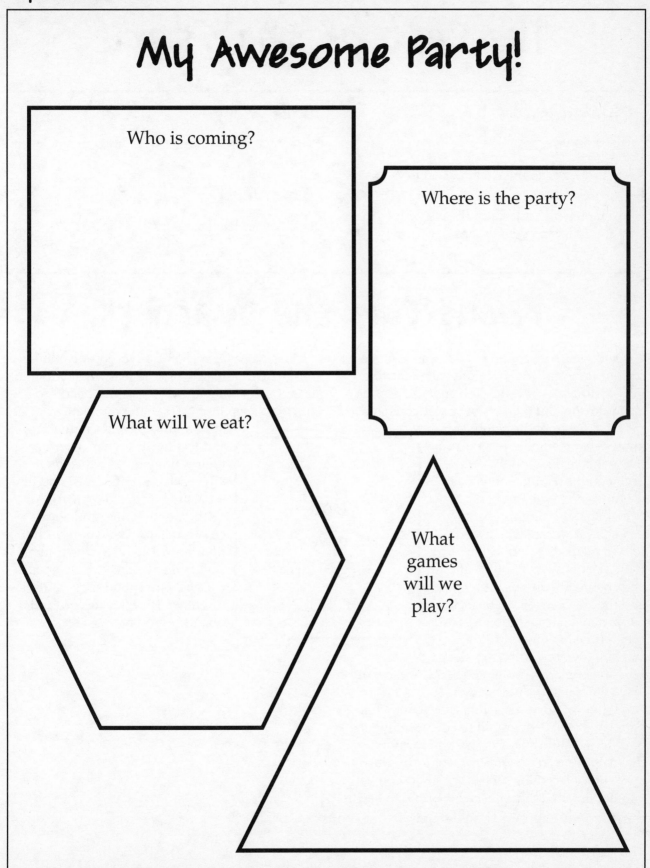

Who is coming?

Where is the party?

What will we eat?

What games will we play?

The Rest of the Story

Objectives

The children will:

- learn what happened after that first Christmas day
- remember that Jesus is always with us in good times and bad times

Bible Story

The Wise Men and the Escape to Egypt
Matthew 2:1-15

Bible Verse

I will never leave you or abandon you.
(Hebrews 13:5*b*)

Focus for the Teacher

Don't you hate coming to the season finale of your favorite TV show? You watch the time ticking down toward the end, and you beg for some closure, but then it's over and you have to wait a few months before you know what really happened. You know that feeling, don't you? You might feel a little of that as we move on to the rest of the Christmas story in this lesson.

Let's see, where were we? Joseph made it to Bethlehem with Mary. Jesus was born safe and sound. Shepherds visited, and the angels rejoiced. But what happened next? Did the shepherds spend time hanging out at the stable? How long did Mary sleep after those energy-draining days? Did the family leave the stable the next day?

Matthew 2 gives us a little clue about what happened next. Joseph and his new family may have moved into a house, and at some point the magi showed up with gifts for Jesus. But just when everything seemed great, Joseph had another dream. In this one, he was told to flee to Egypt with his family to keep them safe.

> God is always with you!

What a roller coaster ride for Joseph and his family! Ups and downs, and just when you think things are settling down…*boom!*…head for Egypt to keep Jesus safe. Can you relate to what Joseph must have been thinking and feeling? Have you ever been rolling along nicely when an unexpected event occurs, and now everything is upside down? I'm betting some of the families in your ministry are dealing with this right now. The Bible tells us that God will never leave us. God is with us in the good times and the bad. It was true for Joseph, and it's true for us today.

Explore Interest Groups

Be sure that adult leaders are waiting when the first child arrives. Greet and welcome each child. Get the children involved in an activity that interests them and introduces the theme for the day's activities.

Star Search

- Hand out **Reproducible–The Rest of the Story: Star Search** to each child. Give children three minutes to count all the stars they can find on the handout. Reveal the answer to the group and see who came the closest.

- Then have children follow the directions on the handout to color the stars.

- After they have finished, bring the children together.

- **Say:** Can anyone tell me who followed a star to find the baby Jesus? *(Allow responses.)* Yes, the wise men. We don't know a lot about the wise men, but we do know they followed a star and came to meet Jesus and give him gifts. Today we are going to learn a little more about the wise men and find out what happened to Joseph, Mary, and Jesus after the first Christmas day.

Make a Gift!

- As children arrive, direct them to the area where you've put the supplies listed in the column to the right. Each child should:
    - o think of a person who lives a long way away who might like to receive a gift
    - o select a note card, decorate it, and write a fun message inside to the recipient
    - o place the card and a piece of candy in the box
    - o wrap the box with some wrapping paper
    - o take the box home and talk to an adult who can help mail the package

- *Note*: Children should feel free to add other items to the box, either during class or when they get home. For example, they might include some leftover candy from other Advent celebrations.

- Once children have finished their packages, bring the group back together.

- **Say:** Can anyone tell us who traveled a long way to see Jesus and brought a gift? *(Allow responses.)* Yes, the wise men! Some people think one of the reasons we give gifts at Christmas time is because the wise men brought gifts to Jesus! We don't know a lot about the wise men, but we do know they followed a star and came to meet Jesus and give him gifts. Today we are going to learn a little more about the wise men and find out what happened to Joseph, Mary, and Jesus after the first Christmas day.

Prepare

- ✓ Supplies needed: red, blue, green, orange, and purple crayons for everyone

- ✓ Go to **Reproducible– The Rest of the Story: Star Search** at the end of this session and make enough copies for everyone to have one.

Prepare

- ✓ Supplies needed: note cards, small boxes, wrapping paper, tape, scissors, candy

Large Group

Bring all the children together to experience the Bible story. Use a bell to alert the children to the large group time.

Prepare

✓ Supplies needed: riddle list, paper and pencil for each team created and for a scorekeeper

Riddle Me This!

- Divide the group into 3-4 teams. Each team selects a spokesperson for their group. Hand out paper and pencil to the spokespersons. You will also need someone to keep score.

- **Say:** Let's see if you're as smart as the wise men. I'll give you a tricky riddle to figure out. After you hear the riddle, talk quietly with your team to come up with an answer. (Don't let the other teams hear you!) The spokesperson will write down the team's answer. When I say so, the spokesperson for each team will hold up their answer. If you get it right, your team will get 1,000 points! Let's see which team can get the most points.

- Read the riddles below. For each riddle, allow a minute or two for groups to discuss and then ask for everyone to hold up their answers. Award points.

  o Q: I'm tall when I'm young and I'm short when I'm old. What am I?
  o A: a candle

  o Q: What has hands but cannot clap?
  o A: a clock

  o Q: What has four wheels and flies?
  o A: a garbage truck

  o Q: What is at the end of the rainbow?
  o A: the letter W

  o Q: What gets wetter the more it dries?
  o A: a towel

  o Q: What has to be broken before it can be used?
  o A: an egg

  o Q: How can a person go eight days without sleep?
  o A: by sleeping at night

  o Q: What is brown and sticky?
  o A: a stick

  o Q: What is blue and smells like brown paint?
  o A: blue paint

  o Q: Why didn't they play cards on Noah's ark?
  o A: Because Noah was standing on the deck.

- At the end of the game, find out who got the most right and give that group a high five!

Bible Story Experience

- This activity uses a teaching method called Ask a Question. You will make a statement, and then the children will respond by reading the question or statement from the list you posted.

  o **Leader**: It was sometime after Jesus was born.

  o **Group**: Christmas was over?

  o **Leader**: Yes! The first Christmas was over, but there were still a few people coming to meet Jesus for the first time.

  o **Group**: Jesus was having more visitors?

  o **Leader**: Yes! Wise men from the east were following a star! These visitors have also been called kings! *(Bring out crowns.)* They wanted to meet Jesus.

  o **Group**: The wise men were following a star?

  o **Leader**: Yes! They traveled a long way to meet little Jesus. And they gave him three gifts.

  o **Group**: Jesus got three gifts?

  o **Leader**: *(Display the 3 gift boxes.)* Yes! The three gifts were gold, frankincense, and myrrh. After the wise men left, Joseph had a dream.

  o **Group**: Not another dream!

  o **Leader**: *(Show the pillow.)* Yes! This dream was a message from God to Joseph.

  o **Group**: God gave a message to Joseph?

  o **Leader**: Yes! It was a very important message. God told Joseph that the baby Jesus was not safe. A bad king named Herod wanted to hurt Jesus.

  o **Group**: Why did Herod want to hurt Jesus?

  o **Leader**: Herod was afraid that Jesus was going to take his place as king. To keep Jesus safe, God asked Joseph to take his new family and travel to Egypt. *(Display the travel bag.)*

  o **Group**: Another trip?

  o **Leader**: Yes! Joseph, Mary, and Jesus had to leave quickly in the middle of the night.

  o **Group**: Were they scared?

  o **Leader**: Yes! I'm sure they were scared, but they were not alone! God was with them and helped them get through that scary time.

  o **Group**: God was with them?

  o **Leader**: Yes! God was with them. And God is with you, too!

  o **Group**: The end!

Prepare

✓ Supplies needed: crowns, three gift boxes, pillow, travel bag, whiteboard or large sheets of paper, something to write with

✓ Before class, write the group portions of the dialogue (at left) on a whiteboard or on large sheets of paper, then post these where the group can see and read them. Don't write out or post the leader statements.

The Rest of the Story

- Discuss these questions:
  - o Why do you think the wise men traveled so far to see Jesus?
  - o Before this session, did you know that Joseph, Mary, and Jesus had to escape to Egypt after that first Christmas?
  - o How do you think Joseph felt as they left in the middle of the night?

- **Say:** On a dark night sometime after Christmas, Joseph packed up his family and quickly got out of town. They probably had a torch or candle to guide their way. I'm sure this was not what Joseph wanted. He didn't want to leave at night and go to another country, but to keep Jesus safe Joseph knew he had to follow God's instructions. Joseph knew that God was with him every step of the way. God had been with Joseph this whole time!

God Is With Us

- **Say:** Today we've learned that after Christmas, Joseph had some tough things to deal with. He learned that Jesus was in danger, and so they had to run away to Egypt in the middle of the night. But God was with them, and they were able to make it through.

- **Say:** Like Joseph, we will also have tough things to deal with in our lives. If we haven't had a hard day or even a hard week, someday we will. We'll feel scared or worried like Joseph.

- Hold up the inflated balloon without water in it.

- **Say:** This balloon is a boy named Bob. Bob has been having a hard day. *(Light the candle.)* Let's have this candle be the hard day Bob is having. What are some hard things that might be happening to Bob? *(Accept responses.)*

- **Say:** Well, Bob thinks he'll be just fine and doesn't need help from anyone or even from God. Watch what happens to Bob during his hard day.

- Hold the balloon by the knot. Lower the balloon above the flame, and the balloon will pop.

- **Say:** Bob's day just got worse.

- Pull out the second balloon, the one that has water in it.

- Don't worry, Bob is back. Only this time, when Bob has a hard day he remembers that God is with him and can help him through the day. So inside this balloon, I have some water, and the water will represent God. It's a reminder that God is with Bob. This time when Bob has a hard day, he prays to God and asks for strength. Now watch what happens when I put the balloon back over the fire again.

- Place the balloon over the flame for just a few seconds. The water keeps the balloon from popping. (Don't hold the balloon over the flame for too long!)

- **Say:** Even when God is with us, we will still have hard times— just like Bob the balloon and just like Joseph. But we can make it through those hard times when we remember that God is with us.

Prepare

- ✓ Supplies needed: tall candle, candle holder, two balloons, water, marker, candle lighter

- ✓ Set up the candle in the candle holder.

- ✓ Inflate one balloon, tie it off, and draw a face on it with the marker. Be sure the knot is at the top of the face.

- ✓ Add some water to the second balloon, then inflate it. Draw the same face on it.

- ✓ You'll want to practice this activity before doing it in front of the children.

Small Groups

Divide the children into small groups. You may organize the groups around grade levels or around readers and nonreaders. Keep the groups small, with a maximum of ten children in each group. You may need to have more than one group at each grade level.

Prepare

✓ Supplies needed: blank paper, markers, bad day descriptions, Bible

Younger Children (Grades K–2)

- **Say:** Everything seemed to be working out for Joseph. He and Mary had made it to Bethlehem safely. Jesus was born. Shepherds had come to visit. Wise men had brought gifts for Jesus. But then Joseph had another dream, and God spoke to him in the dream. God told Joseph that Jesus was not safe, and the family would have to run away to Egypt. I don't know about you, but that would make me a little scared and really ruin my day. But Joseph remembered that God was with them, so they did not have to be afraid.

- Hand out a sheet of paper and some markers to each child. Ask them to divide the paper into four segments on each side, using a marker.

- **Say:** All of us have bad days. Hard things happen to make us feel scared, angry, sad, or hurt. It won't be the same as what Joseph experienced, but God will still be with us. I'm going to read you a few descriptions of bad days. After you hear the description, draw a picture of your face that shows how you might feel in that situation. You will only have 90 seconds, so you'll have to draw the face quickly. Put each face in a different box on your paper.

- Read the statements below. After each one give the children 90 seconds to draw how they would feel in that situation, then have the children hold their pictures in the air.
  - o Your best friend at school is moving away.
  - o Someone you care about is sick.
  - o You get to spend the day with your best friend.
  - o Instead of playing with your friend tomorrow, you have to go shopping with your mom.
  - o Your teacher gives you a lot of homework.
  - o Your lunch at school is a ham sandwich with broccoli on the side.
  - o A storm cancels your basketball game.
  - o You remember that God is always with you.

- **Say:** What you need to know is that no matter how good or how bad your day might be, no matter how scared or happy you feel, God is always with you. Joseph remembered that as he went from good times (celebrating Jesus' birth) to hard times (having to run away to keep Jesus safe).

- Close with a prayer. You can pray, a child can pray, or someone can read the prayer below.

  Dear Lord, thank you that you are with us all the time on good days and bad days. Please give us the strength to follow you even when things don't go according to plan just like Joseph did. In Jesus' name. Amen!

Faithful: Children's Leader Guide

Older Children (Grades 3-6)

- To begin, it might be fun to read a portion of the story *Alexander and the Terrible, Horrible, No Good, Very Bad Day* by Judith Viorst. This would be a great way to get the children thinking about what a bad day looks like in their world.

- **Say:** We all have bad days and even bad weeks. Life doesn't always go the way we want it to, as Joseph found out in our story today. Let's make a list of things that would make a bad day for all of us.

- Allow responses, and write them on the whiteboard or large sheet of paper.

- **Say:** This is a great list of bad things! I agree they would all make for a bad day. And the key to getting through bad days is remembering that God is with us and will give us the strength to make it through.

- **Say:** For the next few minutes we're going to make a reminder that since God is always with us, we can bounce back from a bad day! First, we'll make a balloon ball.

- Hand out to each child one balloon, rice, and a funnel.

- Instruct the children to put the rice in their balloons using the funnels. Add enough rice to each balloon so it is almost the size of a small apple.

- Once there's enough rice in a balloon, tie off the balloon.

- Have the child write her or his name and a sad face on the balloon.

- Next, hand each child a bouncy ball, but ask the children not to bounce it yet.

- **Say:** The balloon ball represents us on our bad days. We might feel sad, scared, or worried. To see what that's like, please drop your balloon ball on the ground. *(It will just sit there.)*

- **Say:** We can be like this balloon ball and allow the bad day to keep us down. Or we can be like the bouncy ball in your other hand. When a bad day comes, we can bounce back with God's help! Try it! *(When the children drop the ball, it bounces back.)* Bad days will come, but God is always with us so we can bounce back like a bouncy ball.

- Allow the children to try the two balls a few more times, then hand out the resealable bags to hold both the balloon ball and the bouncy ball.

- **Say:** Keep these two balls nearby, and let them be a reminder that God is with you when something tough happens to you, as it did to Joseph. You can bounce back!

Prepare

- ✓ Supplies needed: whiteboard or a large sheet of paper, something to write with, rice, balloons, funnels, bouncy balls, markers, gallon-sized resealable bags

- ✓ Optional: the book *Alexander and the Terrible, Horrible, No Good, Very Bad Day* by Judith Viorst

- Close with a prayer. You can pray, a child can pray, or someone can read the prayer below.

    Dear God, help us to be like Joseph and bounce back when something unexpected or difficult comes our way! Thank you that you give us the strength to make it through our bad days. In Jesus' name. Amen!

Star Search